To ...
with love a...
for all your...
writer to a...

A CAVE

OF

OVERWHELMING

a collection of poems

by

Cicely d'A. Angleton

A CAVE

OF

OVERWHELMING

a collection of poems
by
Cicely d'A. Angleton

BRITAIN BOOKS
1995

A CAVE OF OVERWHELMING

a collection of poems

by Cicely d'A. Angleton

Published by Britain Books
6719 Tomlinson Terrace
Cabin John, Maryland 20818

Cover Design
Guru Sangat K. Khalsa
Great Falls, Virginia

First Printing 1995

Manufactured in the United States of America.
Library of Congress Catalog Card Number: 95-81111
ISBN 1-882310-02-0

To my children, with love and gratitude
for their encouragement and help

ACKNOWLEDGMENTS

I would like to express my deep gratitude to all my teachers at The Writer's Center and to my classmates who helped with their critiques.

Contents

Contents

III

IV

Contents

V

I

This Is My Body

But is this so unusual?
Here in these northern pines, malevolent,
even on sunny days? I stop my bicycle,
letting my feet drag upon the ground.

Over the carcass of a deer,
bug eyed, stiff legged in a ditch
on the road to Lake Nebagamon,
spotted butterflies drift high and low
like troops of angels
climbing and descending Jacob's ladder.

Fireweed and goldenrod screen the rot
of flesh and entrails coloring the grass.
Nothing blinds the joy of these stoned scavengers
who trapped the scent, stronger and more seductive
than miles of purple clover.

Headed for Milwaukee, a passing truck
rattles to a stop. Holy shit, the driver says,
covering his nose. Get a load of that.
Used to be the sheriff's job.
What gives with these environmentalists?
The truck accelerates and disappears
quick over the hill, one long note
accenting the silence.

Flat feet moving with the quiet tread
of an old priest stealing to the communion rail,
a black bear pads across the road
in my direction. Lickety split

I'm out of there, ice on the handle-bars
scorched by the sun, and over and over
the wheels repeat, Aren't butterflies supposed to be
vegetarian?

Field Happenings

All through my childhood in Wisconsin
I picked blueberries by the road
that winds in easy curves between the river
and the field above our house. That was when
I started listening to trees. Their speech
is difficult. They have no syllables
and the wave lengths are irregular.
They speak in dialect. Pine trees talk
in muffled cadences, like distant freight trains
rounding the shore of Lake Superior.
Paper birch and poplars express themselves
in repetitious whispers, flutter kicks
and water notes confined to upper keys.

Once, bored by their conversation I interrupted.
Did you see Indians in this field, living in tepees?
Explorers portaging birch-bark canoes?
Do you like blueberries?
But the black eyes of the paper birch
looked straight through me. Over their temples
the Norways formed a barricade of silence.
Alien, the alders whispered.
But one branch smelling of ponds and purple clover
brushed my face as I got up to leave.
My name's Willow, said a voice
softer than thistledown. Are you
Nancy?

Brule August

Outside my cabin door I see a snake
stretched like a long green ribbon in the grass.
Paralyzed, we stare at one another. Between his jaws
he grips a frog pop-eyed and motionless, one
ruby drop exactly centered on his head. I blink
and they are gone. Poplars murmur in the wind
and up the road a wood-pecker taps messages.
Back in the house I find some birch
and build a fire.

Even in August you need a fire in these
north woods. I see the wicker rocking chair,
a lamp that needs rewiring. Bats hang
upside down from curtain folds, suspended
until night. They look like withered figs.
On the wall, rubber waders nudge each other
when the kitchen door bangs shut. They're split

like the bamboo rods that flicked
and bent above the Falls at midnight. Like the post
along the fence that made me call your name
one evening after sunset. Maybe
the frog was lucky.

Erosions

Lake Superior wallows in my back yard.
Black chunks of Minnesota earth
dissolve in the receding spray
where tombstones bob for apples and geraniums
planted for Olga Bustrek and Elisabeth
whose graves were once our next door neighbors.
Suffocate their voices. Let the northeaster
bury them or let your fingers
run up and down in scales on the piano.

Our family wrapped their grief in heavy parcels
covered with newsprint from the first
World War. Jerked them with cord, then stacked
the packages down in the basement
under the billiard table. Or piled them
in the attic next to the headless torso
that terrified new friends who came to play
with us. On sad occasions
a ball of string was always rolling
and fish hooks sealed our eyes.

Maybe that's why I made a bee-line
straight for the tear bottles at Grandmother's.
She kept them in a corner cabinet
next to some coral Buddhas and Oriental buckles.
Oval and opaline, they measured high
as my little finger. Once I tried to squeeze
my own fat tears inside an opening but they
slid down my cheeks. These treasures were
for silk kimono goddesses who hid them
in their sleeves under the lacquered shade
of parasols in painted gardens.

What did they have to cry about?
Our gardens were the pit of the Mesabi Range,
the beaches of Lake Superior.
But the mine closed down and the beaches have
disappeared into the lake.

Eli

The mayfly leaves the stream
to be devoured in a single day
by speckled trout or kingfisher
hovering and snapping in the twilight.

You never left the stream.
From our front steps and porches
we observed you, sleeping on your mother's
shoulder while she talked to neighbors.
Watched your buggy's slow ascent
of our suburban hill
and monitored your silence.
I never heard you cry.

Once you smiled at me
and underneath those heavy lids
I saw your eyes
for one split second.
A blue so deep
a star could shine in them.

Ceremonials

Coming from the southwest I get thirsty
whenever I hear psalms or prayers
with green in them. Whenever I hear frogs
celebrating rain.

Once we drove from Tucson north
to the Hopi reservation.
Picnicked in a field of grass and mariposa
lilies drenched in silence.

In the distance, prehistoric monsters
floated toward each other. Look,
my mother said. On that mesa, that's Oraipi
where Hopis dance for rain with rattlesnakes
between their teeth. You cannot take
their pictures. I looked up from movie magazines
and squinted in the sun.
Sure, I said, I guess so.

That night it rained. The Indians got drunk.
And all across the reservation frogs appeared
to gloat in the arroyos.

These fragments I remember
just after sleep when it's impossible
even to lift your eyelids.
Mesas collide with rattlesnakes
and in the grass
Indians and frogs are joined
in sacred dances.

The Revenant

Once you claimed insurance companies
predict an average of eight years
of widowhood. Now you ask
am I enjoying them?
Honey, be serious.
My days are hemmed together in such even seams
they look like linen sheets. Nights
on this great big square deserted slab
I count the feathers in my pillow.
Dream of dead Egyptian kings
stuffed with alabaster plugs in every orifice.
But let me ask you, if we could revive
the rich disorder of our lives:
broken chariots and eyes outlined in black
upon the wall, would either one of us return?

Your silence is disturbing.
You're not the only one
who can adjust to change.

Recollection

Let me confess since you are dead
that sometimes after coming
I saw my face stone cold within the glass,
vipers hissing in the hair
that brushed your cheek.
You turned away or shrugged indifferently.
But other times before the turn
I saw within your eyes
bright and alert to danger
a look as soft as moss along a forest path
or ferns trampled by deer at midnight.

Check-Up At Window Rock

This den smells of foxes. Are those my bones,
those moonlit ocotillo ribs upon the screen
that hums and flashes secret messages?
Is it Hallowe'en already? Does that thick scar
tissue around the heart belong to me?
How many times am I required to give my soul
away? An old bag lady haunting dark places.
If I had cornmeal in this plastic sack
I'd sprinkle it to ward off evil spirits.

Once I tried to scatter cornmeal on a fox
but he retreated into a cave of overwhelming
dark, turning his head to watch me with a look
of singular attention. Golden eyes. A whirr
of wings blotted my mouth, silencing the chant
as I approached him on my knees to make
my offerings. And still he kept his distance.

Why is this magic more powerful than his?
Witchcraft has stolen what he waited for.
If he was an evil spirit, well then, so am I.
Give me the picture, please.
It's a good day to go hunting.

Nunc Dimittis

Who is that red monkey in a visor,
mumbling by my bed?
Are you my mother or my father?
Husband or children?
How should I know in this white light,
in the glare of dying?
But before I find a space
in that great parking lot in the sky,
let me tell you, buddy,
picking up your tennis balls
has been a pleasure.

II

Lord Murray's Daughter

Ten ravens crouched upon the snow.
Sing hi-dee-ho, sing wassail.
Ten black ravens in a row
outside Lord Murray's castle.

And one was black as stormy water.
Of noble plumage, he,
who loved the laird's headstrong daughter,
the rose-lipt Emily.

But another suitor claimed her hand,
of forty years or fifty.
Rich in lineage and land
but cowardly and shifty.

Across the loch, across the moor,
wedding bells rang clear.
The bridegroom pounded at the door.
The bride did nae appear.

She stood beside her lattice sma',
sing hi-dee-ho, sing tara-li.
And listened to the raven's caw
right merrily.

"O mither, father, fare ye well
and bridegroom pale and craven.
For though I travel straight to hell
I'll wed my bonny raven."

Ten steps she took outside the keep,
deep in the snow she shivered.
The raven plucked her in his beak
and flew her through the blizzard.

The mother wept, the father swore,
the bridegroom blew his whistle.
But ne'er saw they the lovers more
in heather time or thistle.

Three Women

Helen

Sweet sister, Clytemnestra, hear my cry
and come to this abandoned seat in Sparta's halls,
leaving the darkness of your bee-hive tomb,
the lion-guarded gates of doomed Mycenae.
Our fates are joined by a single thread.
For I, whose beauty once provoked the gods
and men to war, am now in middle age
held in high scorn and contumely. My husband,
Menelaus, has deserted me for a young slave
from Crete, my handmaiden. Harden my resolve
and guide the hand that kills him.

Clytemnestra

Helen, my poor distracted girl, you ever were
a vain and forward child, dazzled by pleasure's
golden offerings. You miss the point. The bastard
of Apollo's hireling was but a passing whim
unworthy of a queen's most trifling thought.
I killed King Agamemnon not for his soldier's lust
but for my daughter's murder. Slain to change
the course of war. The war you brought upon us.
No will of mine can help you.

Iphigenia

Cool it, mother. Like I keep telling you,
that baby face Aegisthus was the real reason
for your bloody deed. At least my father carried out
a god's command. As for Aunt Helen, she's a silly bitch
but she played hide and seek with me when I was young
in fields of asphodel. Tell her to go to Ithaca
and ask Penelope if she could use another weaver
in her school for village idiots. Leave me in peace.
Besides, I live in California now.

In Arromanches

When that old lady dies, my mother's friend,
I'll say goodbye to Arromanches
the double rainbow of my youth. The Norman rain
will fall from apple trees into her grave
and the low tide will retreat to honor her,
leaving gifts of moss and sea anemone.
Drifting from hedgerows and all along the cliffs
an army of invisible young men
will join the mourners, jostling each other
for a look at somebody who lived so long.
They will consider the raw earth
and silently begin to clean their boots
with the butt end of their guns.

The Monk Of Jumièges

How can I clear the mind of spider webs
that trap the prayers struggling to fly
up to the throne of God and judgment day?
Not all the weighty psalms and canticles
intoned beneath these groined vaults
can crush the memories that cling
tighter than insects to a sticky thread,
recalling Hastings and the English king.

Like that dread comet prophesying doom
shone Harold on the ridge opposing ours.
His shield wall closed around him, so tightly packed
no wounded man could fall. They held aloft
the gold and purple dragon of the Wessex house
and screamed their battle cry. On either side
the low-born fyrd stood fast. Foot-soldiers
repulsed our mounted knights and myriads of archers
with pick-axes and stones. Northumbrians they were
and Wessex thralls who hailed from marshy shires
of fog and shifting winds where wizards dwell
and mumbling crones interpret runes and portents.

Then William, our liege lord, scenting defeat
feigned to desert the field. Shouting and scrambling
into the valley the fyrd pursued our men.
The cunning duke ordered his knights to charge
and gave commands to shoot high overhead.
It looked as if the sun had suffered an eclipse.
The English king fell with an arrow to his eye.
The shield wall broke but only long
after the sun went down.

William is dead and Harold lies unshriven
in his grave. In Jumièges, this Norman graveyard
for my honours lost, my prayers squeak
like bats within a crypt. How then can I atone
for sins already meaningless when memories
of that October day and courage far beyond
the scope of saints still hinder me?

Letter From Alcuin To Peter Of Pisa

Greeting to my dear and pious friend.
Know that your packet has arrived
and with it the first glimpse of spring.

Aachen this winter has been a trial
for old men like myself. No difference
between earth and sky, so much snow
has fallen. Ice cracks the trees
and twigs form jewelled crosses
on the ground. My back is rounder
than a Roman arch from daily labors
in the damp air of the scriptorium.
This draughty palace school of our beloved
Charlemagne is yet another cave of Aelous.
My brother clerics huddle together in their
black and threadbare robes. Indeed, it is hard
to tell them from the crows.

God forgive me but I long for Italy
and the great pagan sun which Horace has restored
like an illumination in a manuscript.
The poem appears intact after a journey
of six months over the Alpine passes.
"Quis multa gracilis te puer in rosa..."
Like the blessed Anthony in Egypt
a demon pulls me by the hair.

Someday I will transcribe the poem
in clear minuscule. But now my cell
is brighter for its presence and my mind
is torn by strange misgivings and exuberance
unworthy of my calling. The forlorn figure
of Our Lord over my bed is mocked
by naked gods rejoicing in their carnal flesh
and green mysterious demesne. On my knees
I am assailed by wanton laughter in echoing
sea caves, lewd outpourings of love.
Husks of prayer and abstinence imperfectly
sustain me, but oh! how painful to behold
the world again through pagan eyes.
Send me no more, at least until next Michaelmas.
These temptations should be borne by younger men.

Outside my window in the dusk a laughing boy
crosses the courtyard. He holds a goose
who pecks at his round cheeks and struggles
to be free. But the boy strokes her neck,
buries his face in feathers, calls her by pet names.
Then like the swallow of the Venerable Bede
they disappear into the dark.

Ora pro nobis et bene vale.

The Weaver's Song

The bells will soon be tolling vespers and the light
fades on the cathedral square. The threads are blurred
upon my loom. One rose is nearly finished for Our Lady.
By Mary's month this cloth will grace the form that leans
compassionate beyond her niche toward sinners
who implore her intercession. Within the rose a cupid's
dart is hidden, small as a thorn. For once a poet held
me in his arms. François he called himself and boasted
that he was Parisian born. Half drunk and shivering
for the December wind blew chill across the square,
he asked to share my pallet for the night. Sur le Noël,
he murmured, morte saison. I covered his thin shoulders
with my cloak and his dark face smiled at me. I have
not a sou to pay but I can give you love.

Night long he kissed me sweetly and once he swore
my eyes were bluer than the skies of Avignon.
I laughed and said my eyes were green.
He held a candle to them and declared
that never was such green in Normandy
nor in milady Laura's trailing gown.
At dawn he left, teeth chattering from the cold.
Never again did I behold him here in Amiens.
Some say he died twisting the hangman's noose.
Now may our Lady in her rose embroidered mantle

plead for him instead of me on Judgment Day
and sing to him full joyously
in her walled garden underneath blue skies
in far-off Paradise.

Ever After

Remote and distant as Jerusalem
the gentle kiss and my awakening.
Except the scream of terror when I saw
all my joys dissolving into day.
As in a dream I married the young prince
who braved the thorns to rescue me.
Indifferently watched children grow
and move away. Finished the tapestry
that hangs in shreds over the banquet hall
as retainers mourned my husband's death
in wars beyond the sea. An old woman now

I live alone, imperfect in my mind.
Yet certain that this world, where spirit
wars with flesh, is meaningless when I recall
the magic experienced in sleep. Even today,
after long intervals, beloved forms
rise and fall in scattered threads of unremembered
light. But dark, increasingly obscure. I am prepared

for death but in my prayers I ask
for one more visit to the vanished tower,
the spiral steps that led to my enchantment;
and pray once more to hold
the blood-stained spindle in my hand.

Suttee

I am married to my childhood. Father,
mother, I thee wed and all the dead
and smiling aunts in linen dresses,
uncles who forgot my name. And I consign
thee to black albums stacked in cobwebs
high above the fireplace. I am murdering

my childhood with crumpled newspaper
and matches. Minnesota's Queen Victoria,
right eye curling in the flames, whose love
warmed you, Duluth's most dignified librarian,
through the iron range of winter nights,
my mother's friend who came to tea on rainy
Saturdays? Curtsy first, then pass the sandwiches.
But once you brought me snow-drops from the woods.
Burn, lady, burn. Better than future laughter.

Enter Prince Hamlet from Minneapolis. Why preserve
this melancholy smile that faded when he shot
himself one spring morning, killing the wild
flowers? What's he to Hecuba or to my children
who will turn the page? Although I still can see
the sun's position in the sky.

Ram, Ram, my fingerprints are smudged over
the fireplace. Consider this unseemly ritual
accompanied by winds chanting from the lake
and the cries of children skipping stones
among the waves.

III

First Sight

One rainy day on Brattle Street my weekend date
walked me up three flights of narrow stairs
to meet his college room-mate.
At the long end of a barely finished room
How do? the young Chicano said politely
melting from El Greco's stormy painting of Toledo
before he disappeared again.
I fell right through the creaky floor-boards,
through damp roses wired to the sidewalk,
past St. Theresa's plaster statue in the garden.
Beware, she warned, of hollow cheeks
and auras sketched in lightning.
That bounced me up again.
Hello I said or didn't say.

Reunion In Pratt

"It's fun," my little brother once remarked,
"to make this stop in Kansas on the train.
I like to see the cars line up
behind the mighty X-s. Hear them honking
at us. I like the water tower big and blue,
with Pratt on it. Someday
I'll come back here with a friend."

His death made that impractical.
If ever I return,
I'll take his ashes neatly stored
beneath my seat
and throw them at the water tower
the only vertical for miles around.
Stuck up on stilts like him
and solitary. Maybe a cotton-wood will grow
and push long roots beneath the tracks.

Then I'll sit back and watch the sky
make room for the descending sun.
Trace the horizon
straight as a lead pencil.
Get even with the stars
that blaze and set and never gave a damn
that he existed.

Getting There

You can keep your cellar door
Minneapolis.
I don't want to play in your yard.
Into it out of it
last stop on the way,
fire escapes crisscrossing
rectangle eyes. Semaphores clicking
danger and stop. Who even
can count the telephone crosses
stringing the prairie?
Dribbling patches of stubble and snow—
old men's faces—Look at the blue
under the fences. Mother, how soon

do we get there? But she's too busy
with my little brother. Not a cool
spot on him night after day. Hate
from her eyes instead of an answer.
So I start counting,
twenty two twenty three:
just give him back to me
right now.

Birthday Child

Now greet the little girls and boys,
and sweet expressions muster.
And share your precious birthday toys,
the blue balloon with Buster.

My darling, if you pin the tail
under the donkey's belly,
then let a cheery smile prevail.
Don't take it out on Nellie.

I've lit the candles one by one.
Now blow and do not splatter
little Tom with icing from
the cake upon the platter.

O shame on you to start a fight.
You've pulled his hair and kicked him.
Birthday parties are a rite
and you're the honored victim.

So take the cake from Tommy's head.
His mother's here to fetch him.
Give him a parting shove instead
and say goodbye to Gretchen.

Envoi

O birthday parties come and go
and some are made in heaven.
But so help me if I ever throw
another one like seven.

Child's Play

In the room where little frogs
dance on the wall and bumble bees
play the piano, a small girl sits
in a lavender smock playing with dolls.

And Bang! up goes mommy straight to heaven.
Daddy stays behind.
And Pow! there goes baby brother
crayon red
torn apart for his candy heart.
Sawdust flies through the air.

The spectator makes encouraging sounds
and writes on her pad, Mary Anne
is an active child who continues to show
signs of significant progress.

New Forms For Old

You wanna change? the geomancer sang
To make a difference? Buy my right angles
short and snappy, great for mid life crisis.
Circles anyone? They turn continually
and stay in place. Hey, grandma, good for your
lifestyle. Straight lines? you, young lady
in the blue beret, they meet in the hereafter.
Mystery that's what I'm selling here.
He paused to wipe his forehead
with a cylinder shaped sleeve.

Middle age, a man stepped forward.
I want to scale the sheer cliff
of the hypotenuse. And at the apex
thumb my nose at winds
that never turn a corner.

Then bring me prayer flags from the walls
of Lhassa, said the grandmother. To flutter
in my Oriental garden. Opium for my insomnia.

A footprint of the white snow leopard,
said the girl, inaudible between her fingers.

You haven't any thumbs, the geomancer said
examining his hands. Only stumps
that look like small parabola.
Frostbite. Here's an hypotenuse for maimed
veterans of the slope.

But will it change me? asked the man.
Transform me into a dead star to radiate
dead visions to a new millennium?
Will I be sucked into that black hole whose mass
no light can penetrate? Who needs thumbs
considering?

Forget it said the geomancer sharply.
I never mess around with time.

Roll down the slope, the young girl
in the blue beret said softly. And slide
downhill to me. I'll give you dinner
and half of my box mattress for the night.

But first, the grandmother advised,
he'll need a bath.

Stop And Go

Hippety hop for failure!
Hippety hop for me.
Gimme your arm my sailor boy
and we'll jiggle across the sea.

Some say this world is for sunshine.
Some say it's for rain.
But I say this world's for falling downstairs
and doing it over again.

Observe the leaves that are dropping
fast from the trees and the sky.
Tell me my lover will they recover
the positions they held in July?

Now lady you take your failure
and whatever you want with it do.
But I can't afford to wash overboard
sailing the ocean blue.

So give me a kiss and promise
to write me in every port.
Where I arrive, the porpoises dive
and lulus in hulas cavort.

Still singing her hymn to failure
she waved him goodbye at the dock.
Well that's over, she said, happy day!
Let's go home and play with the clock.

The clock hasn't ticked for a lifetime.
Its pendulum hangs in a trance.
But she decks it with ribbons and garlands of corn
and sometimes engages in dance.

And for all I know she's still swinging
the second hand this way and that.
The sailor jumped ship in Hawaii,
got married and grew very fat.

But sometimes he looks at his footsteps
diminishing in the sand.
And at the shell of an oyster unable to foster
a pearl for supply and demand.

And he wonders about his sweetie
who championed failure and shame.
She may have been right, he murmurs,
but he can't remember her name.

In Loco Parentis

"Name?" asked the dictionary in a kindly tone
peering through his glasses at the applicant.
"Asterisk your honor if you please.
In English it means little star. Greek I believe."
"I'm aware of that. Your place of origin?"
"At the bottom of the page. That's what they tell me sir."
"Just answer the questions. Family?"
"My father was a footnote. A most impressive character
when he was sober. You might say he suffered from
a multi-personality disorder. Confidential information."
"Completely confidential," said the dictionary
scribbling on his notepad. "And your mother?"
"My mum she wasn't there, most of the time. Kind of
floated in and out of words if you get my meaning."
"Indeed, known as an omission. Were you close?"
"Closer than these rays upon my head," declared
the asterisk. "Her secret sin she called me. Her little
indication. Fondly you know as mothers will."
"I understand. Why do you want to join the company?"
"Personal reasons sir. It's important to belong.
You're an understanding sort of chap. With my
family history wouldn't you risk your ass—"
"Watch your language son. You're out of line."
"Yessir I always am." The dictionary fiddled
with his pencil. "Well, we'll include you.
Put you with the A's. Bring us a photograph
and polish up your rays."

All Things Being Equal

Into the purity of an equation
stumbled an adjective. Man about town
seedy looking, brown around the edges
he smelled unmistakably of drink.
Good lord, said the 9, raising his monocle
what do you think
you're doing here? You're a chronicle
of true disorder. The X-s glared
straightening their spines. The little pye
began to cry, pulling his cap over his eye.
But the zero said, My hero and blushed becomingly.
Now there's a woman for you, said the adjective.
Alive and breathing. Don't worry, I'll be leaving
and thanks for the reception
to your immaculate collection.
Just before he kissed her
he whispered to the zero,
Meet me tonight behind the tall and fluttery
buttery yellow willow tree
and bring a pillow with you.

Well, Maybe

Give me a square on clean white paper
drawn with a cedar pencil #2,
all angles calculated to perfection.
There I can squat or jump from point to point
or run to the middle playing hide and seek
hooting to my companions.
How can you play such games within a circle?
And if my world collapses there'll be one
straight line to cling to. But broken curves
and wavy lines deflect and vacillate,
two steps ahead or two lagging behind.

In spite of eggs and Christopher Columbus
I do believe the world is square
at least on paper yes.
Even though I sometimes spot a rope
that swerves and lunges like a snake
circling the angles.
Pick up the slack, Mac, says a curly voice
who do you think you're kidding?

Night And Day

Brenda Diana Duff Frazier
in that grand Waldorf Astoria in the sky
do you remember me and all the other
thorny cactus country girls in the 11th grade,
your Arizona fan club 1939?
Night and day you were the one
and only glamour girl before the war.
We wrote you letters elaborately polite
asking for autographs and tips
on how to act with boys at parties.
Adopted dark red lipstick and a weary manner.
Saved your cover on Life magazine
and snaps at El Morocco and the Stork Club
where you sat at little gilded tables
surrounded by young men lighting your cigarette
remote as Cassiopeia's chair.

What happened to those young men?
Did they step off the elevator
at Anzio and Tarawa
stubbornly refusing to return?
Are they waves pounding deserted beach-heads?
jungle insects trailing one another single file?

You stayed the same
diamonds and expression interchangeable.
But forever after
you looked a little smaller.

The cactus country Arizona fan club
soon dissolved. We lost some thorns,
grew new ones for protection. In those days
you grew up in a hurry.

The Bad Child

Naughty naughty at the table.
Spit at cook and spit at Mabel
passing peas and smashed potatoes
buttered crumbs and squashed tomatoes.

When it's time for saying grace
hold your tongue and make a face.
Drop your retainer in the dish
normally reserved for fish.

And when sternly sent to bed
think of all you should have said.

Fission Vision

Three notes dancing
before my very eyes
a disembodied jig
to a deaf man's penny whistle.

Will you please call a raven
from that square church tower
to pluck them from the pellicle
with his surgical
beak?

And I'll leave four plump raisins
under the chinaberry tree
or maybe peanut butter
to keep his mouth shut.

To Johnny

You promised me a ribbon
from the country fair.
Instead you bought a gibbon,
an ape with furry hair.

And he may be the missing link,
a jewel in his fashion.
But he swings around the kitchen sink
and eyes me with a passion.

While you carouse in foreign ports,
to heathen isles set sail,
he frolics in unseemly sports
and brandishes his tail.

His howling awakes the dead.
The neighbors are complaining.
He's better when he stays in bed
especially if it's raining.

And I am leaving, oh my dearie,
with you in far Cathay.
When you return to Eire
I'll be long away.

A note upon the dairy
you'll read with bitter rue.
So haste and do not tarry:
of gibbons there are two.

Hallowe'en

Take a smoking candle
and trace the first three letters of your name
upon the handle of the crescent moon.
Then as the night grows colder
with a silver spoon
throw salt across your shoulder
and cry Avaunt thee!
and I won't haunt ye
til you're older.

Cain And Abel

Let a shark's clean bite divide them.
These freaks. Unseparated twins
that roil my sea. Give to one free play
to leap across the prows of ships,
communicate with angels,
rescue drowning sailors.

Let the other burn on the horizon.
Or plunge into a Spanish galleon
shifting the cargo in its hold.

IV

For Elderly Ladies

Brush your teeth with premarin
hormone pearly white.
Shove the toothpaste up the hole.
Get ready for the night.

Eye drops on the typo
whiteout on the eye.
Just remember it's December
Winter's in July.

Farting's such sweet sorrow.
Must you go so soon?
Squeeze the muscle
while you hustle
from the dining room.

In conclusion, seniors,
polish up these skills.
Count your blessings
while undressing
but always count your pills.

January Thoughts

In winter when my cherry tree
blooms overnight, disrespecting April,
I like to shake the boughs for snowballs
and pelt the wan sun
loitering on the edges of the sky
like a bad boy in a schoolyard
before sullenly retreating
under a cloud.

Lexie, On Her Blindness

When you're blue you can't see nothin.
I don know my eyes was so condemned.
Would you have a drink of water, miss?
I think that was very wonderful
for you to sacrifice yourself
an get on over here. Think you like
my place pretty good. This lady here,
she takes care of me when I'm down
an I say gimme a piece of candy
an I eats candy for a while.
But I can hear em callin and hollerin
from here to Alexandria.
I want some pair of shoes.

Tit For Tat

He was a fussy, querulous old scholar,
a philosopher, not your blue collar
type, who wrote brainy and pristine
essays for a classy magazine.
He had a cat
whom a friend once threw
his glassa whiskey at.
And that was that.
They never spoke again.

But Tom found Sallie
after his retreat
to a backyard alley
fence. She was in heat
and with the moon above
they celebrated love.

The Smoker's Ballad

Come gather round this grassy mound
ye smokers brave and true.
Though I am gone and in the ground
I have a tale for you.

When I shed this mortal clay
I wandered up to heaven.
Stopped for a smoke along the way
and got there after seven.

They dragged me to the judgment throne.
It seemed like He was sleeping.
But He looked and gave a heavy groan.
The angels fell to weeping.

I hemmed and hawed and hung my head
and promised to do better.
He pointed to my chest and said,
What's that beneath your sweater?

Give me a puff. I've had enough
of virtue and entreating.
I'm getting old and heaven's cold
and time it is a-fleeting.

We went to hell to find a pub
and gambled there with sinners.
And all of them smoked like Beelzebub
and all of them were winners.

Got so hot we had to stop.
The sulfur singed my hair.
Time to go, He said and so
it's back to harp repair.

Now listen folks I'm outta smokes.
Bring some when you're ready.
What I like is Lucky Strike:
just ring and ask for Freddy.

Desert Seminar

Sumptuously coiled the rattlesnake
basked on a mountain ledge that overlooked
a dusty circle in a parched arroya
where all the desert representatives
assembled for their first seminar
on self esteem.

My problem, said the Gila monster,
blinking his sleepy eyes in the shadow
of a mesquite tree, is slow motion.
When I'm hungry—(here the gophers
streaked back into their holes)—I try
to gather steam. Quite discouraging.
Sometimes they laugh at me.

You need a fat farm, said the ocotillo,
stretching her skinny arms to display
her scarlet fingernails.
They're starting one in Hermosillo.
Especially for reptiles.

The mountain roused herself from apathy.
Diamond Jim, you're smothering my sunshine.

Toothless fossil from a prehistoric age
hissed the rattlesnake. Who gave you authority—?
but he slithered from the rock,
rattling his tail.

No, no, stay where you are,
cried all the others.
You're a picture-book of desert synthesis.

Your problem, breathed the centipede,
raising his front legs in respectful admonition,
is no feet. And so you suffer from too little
exercise and lack of circulation. A well-known
factor in depression.

Myself, I have no problem, whispered the scorpion
emerging from a mica blinded stone.
Each summer night I raise my tail
to my own constellation.

But your color, chirped a pyrrhuloxia,
preening his feathers on a prickly pear.
Have you ever considered eating raisins
for that waxy pallor?

The mountain rumbled for attention.
I must admit my memory has lately been
unfortunate. I can remember my beginnings
and often dream in the Jurassic language.
But as for yesterday—what has happened
to the ocean that sparkled at my feet?

Ocean? said the others, what is an ocean?
But the mountain was asleep and didn't answer.

Scratching The Surface

About an hour ago I lost the spinach.
Just put it down somewhere all brightly packed,
sparkling with malice. Losing your temper
I can understand. Or your faculties.
I lost them long ago by asking questions
at Catholic University.

But this makes me drum my fingers on the table.
Streak lipstick on my cheeks.
And when I find my enemy I'll eat it raw
like flesh devoured by a hostile tribe.
Too bad it doesn't have a heart like lettuce.
I'd eat that last in chicken broth
to make me less forgetful.

Preparations

Thursday, foolish ineffectual old hasbeen,
caught between loose ends and raw beginnings,
is my favorite. Time to wash my hair.
Do the tablecloth forgotten in the basement.
Pine for lost loves. Prepare a mood for Sunday.

How can I love a body with so many wounds?
Appear to me in Cana in white samite,
dancing. We'll drink your wine from terra
cotta bowls and sing, arms linked together,
as the bridegroom turns to kiss
the warm lips of the girl who laughs beside him
and throws away her veil.
Appear to me on Thursday.

To Faustus

Come on, old friend, let's strike a bargain.
Helen waits for you in Ilium.
I'll sell my car and you can buy
a quick parole from Mephistopheles
and practice magic with computer chips.
So many souls on the exchange these days
he's broke and needs the cash.
Retrieve your vision. And in return
transform me into a pink cliff
reflecting sunrise. Some place in northern
Arizona where thunderheads herd sheep
and rattlesnakes hunt in moonlight.
Not my home-town high on a starry lake
where a paralyzed old lady
was smothered for a sapphire on her finger.
At night all cats are grey.

I want time out. Time to change my blood
for sedimentary veins within a rock
(lava or sandstone) until the term expires.
Come visit me—there, you see, I haven't quite
accepted metamorphosis—and you might find
more magic than you ever learned
since Wittenberg.

V

Lente, lente, currite
noctis equii
Christopher Marlowe
Dr. Faustus

Noctis Equii

My grandchildren are sleeping two doors away
in this hotel spawned on the piazza.
Contented with their bodies
they wear whatever suits them for the night.
Victoria's Secret for the teen-ager,
a Humphrey Bogart rain-coat for her younger
brother, second hand and twice too big for him.
Beside them on a mattress my daughter sleeps,
lost in the 60's and pot parties in dorms
where couples lie on sofas in the dark
discussing recipes for squash.

Alone, I feast on bitter almonds
and blue rings floating from the ash-tray.
Have I become a chaperone in my old age?
My fingertips are numb from counting suitcases
and Prego and Grazie trail after me
like starving cats. My biggest thrill
comes in the morning at the cashier's cage
changing base paper into gold.

American Express I am not worthy,
but take the checks only.

Bang goes the tower clock three times,
each measured interval a panic episode.
Slowly, slowly, horses of the night,
and give me time, not to repent like Faustus
but to invoke the magic power of sleep.
Below my window a merry company
celebrates the stars. O stars
turn into meteors and strike them dead.
Boiling water is too good for them.

At the ebb tide of the night I prod the shutters
to see pale minions polishing the tables.
And one, younger and livelier than the rest,
begins to sing. I want to pound the shutters.
Caro, ragazzo, sing to me about Sorrento.
Turn to me and I will rain
green cards upon your head. And jasmine.

My passport tells me that Venetian nights
are not for Minnesota grandmothers.
I'm stuck securely in the 40's. A green canoe
jammed on a rock. Down by the meadow in an iddy
biddy pool fwam fwee little fiddies and mamma fiddy—

too inattentive to listen as the clock
mangles the hour I feel my heart-beat quietly resume
its normal Sunday walk. Content, I pour a drink
and settle back to plan the next excursion.

A Senior Citizen Views An Odalisque At The Art Gallery

Oh pheromones where art thou fled
ye nymphs of rare persuasion?
Out the window, good as dead,
to slaves of smooth Eurasian
belly rolls and ample thighs.
Smoldering exotic eyes
softly say, Come hither baby
before I get like that old lady.

Nativity

More sensitive to threat than angel eyes
guarding a drowsy baby
two round composites bulge and revolve
in all directions. Transparent wings
expand and close on unresponsive forms
contemplating loss. Eyelash thin
six hairy legs explore the mother's
melancholy smile. A long proboscis
taps her lips. Still unappeased, the visitor

retreats to settle on the cheek
of a perspiring tourist
whoslapshimdead
while she explains
why Botticelli
never really grabbed her.

Autumn

Chrysanthemums
huddled together on a bank
like sheep in rain
almost persuade me to wear black
and practice fugues upon a clavichord
inside my closet
while one bar of light
lies flat beneath the door.

Fontana Muta

They have stolen the air, the final souvenir,
the strangers who were here before.
And the dead light of a vacant hotel bedroom
in an unfamiliar city
seals the counterpane, immaculate
within its geometric space. Petrifies the arms
and legs of painted furniture. Hermetically
enclosed, nothing speaks to me. The porter
drops the suitcases and pulls the curtains
lead weight and plum colored, and with a bow
accepts his tip and leaves the door half open.
Through the brown margin I can count
leftover breakfasts heaped on trays
beside a silent regiment of doors.
Are they making love in there?
Sleeping it off?
What if I knocked on all the doors? Permesso,
they're waiting for you in the touring bus outside.
I open the window. For all I care
the Duomo is an old department store
in Superior, Wisconsin.

Perhaps this is the year when women of my age
retreat to boarding houses on a quiet street
where widows eye each other in the dining room
uneasy birds upon a feeder. Cheep cheep
chit chat yes yes much violence in America.
Ma si the Mafia, anche in Italia. Stony resignation
and fatigue engrave their faces. Etruscan tombs
with-holding secrets from the curious.

Not yet that bourne. This traveler can still return
in tennis shoes to bloody dawns and sunsets
insinuating change. And with this pocket book
yanked from my shoulder that whomps upon the bed
regurgitating passport, pocket dictionary, coins
and directions scrawled on torn postcards.
Currents of delicate Botticelli air floating
from crowds beneath the window separate the music
of a street musician from their voices
and bells of bicycles. To the ragged wheezing
of an old accordion he sings about a ruined
fountain that has ceased to play

and I slam into the ceiling short circuiting
the tarnished chandelier. Collapse upon the purse
because I know the song but with the years
have buried it in my own Etruscan style.
The room becomes a danger zone, a ruined balcony
which I invade to throw fountains of coins and paper
lire at the street musician who looks up at me and smiles,
the smile of a friend after a long separation.

No Traveler Returns

Move over, Ophelia, in the water.
I too would drown myself.
What are you doing here in Venice
so far from Elsinore
surveyed by Moorish arches and leprous
iridescent walls? Perhaps rejected love
finds many outlets to oblivion.
Open the petals of your eyes and look at me.
I think you have brown eyes.
My enemy has none.
Just slits within ground glass and porcelain
that follow me from every rounded bridge,
from every bell tower that tolls for noon.
Especially I dread the noon hour
when the black death claimed so many.
My twin, my poor unholy twin,
likes yellow sunlight.
Opaque, who can find me?
Not gondolas nor the masked man
bent to his oar. And yet how cold
this water is and insolent.
Lend me your eyes poor lady,
to wear like amber on my forehead
so I can seek my demon
just as the sun goes down.

Losses

It's no use travelling anymore.
Since sleep has chosen to desert me
why swallow pills or thrash around
in Agra, Tel-Aviv or Foix?
I want to lie in my own bed
where I can see the clock's uneven fingers
steadily describe the cycles of the night.

Then I review my losses. Sometimes
they're mercenaries, hangdog and dispirited,
who spit and urinate against the wall.
Or condors from the Andes.
They fly at me with open beaks,
beating their wings that smell of snow
and traces of blood sacrifice.

The sharp staccato of my neighbor's dog
disperses them. I sit upright
and listen for the slap of paper
against brick. What a comfort to be vertical
and in your own surroundings.

Chrysoberyl

Deep within the cat's eye
my love winks at me.
Sly and lascivious
a true coupling of eyelids.
Unexpected. Like the time
he pinched my bottom at a party
when I was passing the potatoes.

Honey I say blowing off the dust
from dead filing cabinets, ragged
cardboard boxes. What you doing
down there? You're supposed to be
in Idaho six feet under.

Another wink equally distracting.
I spit upon the eye
polish it on the short hairs
rub the stone between my palms.
Blood-stains smear the surface
tasting of ambrosia when I lick them off.

My palms still bleed at vacant intervals.
What do I do now?
Father I've acquired the stigmata,
Shall I wear a hair shirt?
Do twenty lashes?
Am I a saint?

Do not disturb yourself my daughter.
Go home and take a cooling shower
with all your clothes on.
Such hallucinations often trouble
women of your age.

A Benediction

Now blessings on all bad husbands
while one drop of charity
remains in me.
Quick
before the hot wind
blows from the south.

Umbra

I have seen moonlight still the alders on the river,
balsam and cedar, maple and white pine.
And solunar tables warn that a full moon
keeps brown and rainbow trout from feeding
on clouds of mayflies rising from the hatch.
So fishermen stay home at night to patch
their rubber waders. Drink whiskey and tie flies
of gossamer on steel hooks almost invisible. But one

late August night we anchored our canoe
beneath a meteor deserted sky
to watch a full eclipse. The sentient air
was free of mayflies and no bird called
from either side, when shadows blotted out the moon
as quietly and irreversibly as once I saw
a dying man stop breathing.

Vesuvius

Did you come? the man asks. Are you happy?
She kicks the sheets high into the air.
What do you think? Hey, the man says, watch
the ash tray. You're a real volcano. He puts out
his cigarette. Bums up, he says, and rolls away
but she stays on her back and listens to the rumbling
trucks outside their house and flapping window blinds
that in uneven intervals reveal a long procession
of transparent moons and ruby blurs across the walls.

Is there life after intercourse, she wonders. Will
the trashmen come tomorrow? take the ashes from
the fireplace neatly stacked in paper bags like relics
from an ancient site? In another life

I could have been a slave girl buried in lapilli
beneath a long red plaster wall covered with dancing
forms receding into night. Carbonized before she reached
the sea, beside the child in her arms. Do I

want to lie next to this person after death? Even
in cinders he's perfectly capable of goosing me
right through those damn geraniums, those ruby blurs
across the wall. Will I reach the sea where wind and ash
set fire to the waves?

Honey, the man says, turning over. Are you crying?
What's the matter?
I'm thinking of the trashmen, she replies.
For chrissake, he mumbles, Save your tears for tax
returns. I have to work tomorrow.

The Louis Streak

I close my eyes to pray
for peace in the family, peace
to the departed souls who lived and died
in that deserted house sheltered
by mountain ash. Instead, I see a dog

or someone very like a spaniel
cowering on a second story window sill
of spinach green. Downcast eyes
and mouth that trembles when he hears my name.
A little bird says,
Pat him.

It must be Uncle Louis, my easy-going
father's oldest brother because a lamp
goes out the moment that I lift my arm
and always he has feared electricity.
He knows my name, a rare distinction
for uncles in the family.

Wondering if he has bathed
I pat his shoulder. Murmur praises
for his scientific gifts, the calendar
that won first prize at the World's Fair
in Chicago, 1933. He never lifts his eyes

but I can feel electric impulses
gathering momentum. Your father
he whispers with a timid smile,
did he have many enemies?

Sky Watch

The old woman is frightened by the clock.
Which hand is the important one?
She picks it up and carefully observes
a radiant 4:30. Over the garden
Orion freezes in the mild November sky
and she stumbles barefoot to the window
like a supplicant in the presence of a holy man
seeking liberation. It has been

too easy, this eiderdown of silence in a house
where she has lived alone for many years.
The single isolated eye, the pillows
huddled closer on the bed than children
watching TV after dinner. I belong there,

she tells the constellation, in that black
garden, digging for roots that dare not be
disturbed so deep within the earth.
Hunting for arrowheads chipped from obsidian
and eyes fixed on a vanishing point that holds
no memory of me.

After Albuquerque

Flat on my motel bed and hyper-ventilating
who can I call ten minutes after midnight?
So much yellow silence has exhausted me
and the horizontal line of mesas plugged
into the blue and yellow eye of afternoon.

Outside my window the scorpion moon crawls
to the west and from the ceiling bulb
light falls in one long vertical to pluck
eyes from their sockets, marrow from my bones.

Oh zip code man, I gasp into the telephone.
Give me the zip code for Brule, Wisconsin
where rain-clouds like a band of desperadoes
hold up the sun and windy, needle-pointed
pines avert catastrophe.

Yes ma'am, 54820. Mighty good fishing up there
in Wisconsin. Good night now and have a good evening.

And all the blue and yellow weight of silence
changes to the rippling confusion
of a rise of speckled trout
leaping for mayflies.

I Love You, Emily Dickinson

Jenvy and Ellasy, my twin sisters,
came to my house for tea
in high buttoned boots and rustling skirts
that gleamed like ebony.

They kissed my cheeks and searched for lines
that would betray my years.
Said it was undignified
to pierce my ears.

I seated them in antique chairs
covered in thin brocade.
They looked askance upon the silk,
declaring it was frayed.

The pretty fire of paper birch
smouldered in the grate.
I laid my best embroidered cloth
and trembling, cut the cake.

The knife, they said, that silver knife
belonged to Uncle Keith.
They polished the initials
with a linen handkerchief.

And as they chattered I grew mute,
and paler than a nun.
Watched a spider weave her web.
How craftily she spun!

Fast within the web a fly
struggled to be free.
Oh God, I thought, if only I
had so much energy.

The King's Mistress

Inside a closet lined with crepe
I'm peeping through a knothole
to watch a lady bathing. Her hair,

embellished by a rose, is pulled
high from her forehead, one finger
elegantly pointed to a nipple.

The bathtub is too short for full
immersion. She sits, discoursing gravely
on the rules for courtly love

to winsome gentlemen who stand and bow
before her, flowering in ruffles
and expensive lace.

No room here for convoluted daydreams
richly stained by rage and loss,
balanced by soap and water.

What lovers did I ever dare
to woo me in a bathtub?
Stealthily

I touch my eye, glowing in the knothole.
Blind it in crepe
and listen to the soft

light-hearted laughter,
the rustling of bees
squandering the honeycomb.

Observing Squirrels

What circus artists on a high trapeze
can entertain with such electrifying leaps,
show biz chatter, runs and casual displays
of plumed extravaganza? These travelling

performers rev up the fat slow days of summer's
end, this cautious interlude and waiting game,
deliberate as a pregnant woman
maneuvering her way to bed
after a pee at midnight.

Must Come Down

Original sin and ancient Rome
and index cards in shoe boxes
careening from my desk toward
Newton's apple rolling on the floor.
I am so tired of fallen things.
Transom glass over my back door
shattered by a baseball. I need
some panacea to the law of gravity,

and so I say, lowering my eyes,
pick up the apple and enjoy. Kick
the shoe boxes hard beneath the chair.
And Rome, she had it coming.
But cover the fallen angel
tenderly with broken glass.